LILIAN BLAND

LILIAN

H
HERITAGE

BLAND

AN AMAZING AVIATRIX

WRITTEN BY

HALEY HEALEY

ILLUSTRATED BY

KIMIKO FRASER

Heritage House Publishing Company Ltd.
heritagehouse.ca

Cataloguing information available from Library and Archives Canada
978-1-77203-433-2 (hardcover)
978-1-77203-468-4 (paperback)
978-1-77203-434-9 (ebook)

Illustrated by Kimiko Fraser
Cover and interior book design by Setareh Ashrafologhalai

The interior of this book was produced on FSC®-certified, acid-free
paper, processed chlorine free, and printed with vegetable-based inks.

Heritage House gratefully acknowledges that the land on which
we live and work is within the traditional territories of the Lkwungen
(Esquimalt and Songhees), Malahat, Pacheedaht, Scia'new, T'Sou-ke,
and W̱SÁNEĆ (Pauquachin, Tsartlip, Tsawout, Tseycum) Peoples.

We acknowledge the financial support of the Government of
Canada through the Canada Book Fund (CBF) and the Canada Council
for the Arts, and the Province of British Columbia through the
British Columbia Arts Council and the Book Publishing Tax Credit.

27 26 25 24 23   1 2 3 4 5

Printed in China

Illustrations inspired by original images courtesy of: City of Vancouver
Archives (CVA 586-1360, Out P613); http://www.lilianbland.ie;
and University of British Columbia Library, Rare Books and Special
Collections (Lilian Bland fonds, RBSC-ARC-1792-PH-604).

NOTE OF TRUTH AND RECONCILIATION

This book was written on the traditional territory of the Snuneymuxw First Nation. Some of the story takes place on the traditional territory of the Gwat'sinux First Nation. The author fully and completely supports truth and reconciliation and recognizes her own role in truth and reconciliation.

LILIAN was born a long time ago in southern
England. Her mother died when she was
young. Lilian spent her childhood travelling
the world with her father. More than anything,
she wanted to be free and to live her own way.

When she was older, she moved to Ireland and
got a job as a sports journalist. She wrote about
racing cars, hunting on horseback, and how to fall
off a horse without getting hurt.

In those days, most women rode horses side saddle. It was considered more proper. But Lilian insisted on riding like the men. Not everyone liked this. One day, a man on the street saw Lilian riding her horse. He told others to throw stones at Lilian for not riding the proper way.

But instead, people took Lilian's side. They cheered for her as she rode by!

Lilian loved trying new things. She wanted to fly like the black-backed seagulls soaring over the ocean.

She dreamed of flying a plane, but she couldn't find anyone to teach her.

So, she set to work, designing and building her own plane!

Using her uncle's workshop, she used spruce, bamboo, and canvas to build a glider plane with twenty-foot wings.

She bought a lightweight engine and put everything together. She changed the design again and again before she was satisfied.

Lilian named her plane *Mayfly* because it may or may not fly. *Mayfly* was similar to the first plane ever flown, which was built by the Wright Brothers seven years earlier. But *Mayfly* was Lilian's own design.

One day in August, it was finally time to
see if *Mayfly* would lift off. Lilian launched off
the ground.

It flew! Lilian soared and admired the fields
below from a new view. She had never felt so
free. Lilian was the first woman in the world to
design, build, *and* fly her own plane!

After her first flight, Lilian kept working on *Mayfly*. She made several more flights. She even built biplanes and gliders and sold them to others.

But after a while, Lilian grew restless. She became more interested in cars than planes. She started running a car dealership and married a man named Charles. But she still didn't feel free.

So, Lilian and Charles moved to Canada. They bought some land, deep in the wilderness of northern Vancouver Island, in a place called Quatsino Sound. This was the traditional territory of the Quatsino (Gwat'sinux) First Nation, who had lived there for thousands of years.

Lilian and Charles's new home was far from any big cities. No roads went there. To get there, Lilian and Charles had to travel by a big steamship.

On the way, they passed a rocky island with a lighthouse. Even through the wind and waves, the light shone through. Lilian spotted sea lions and sea birds. The birds reminded her of the gulls that had made her want to build and fly her own plane.

At their new home, Lilian and Charles built a cabin, a farm, and gardens. They had a daughter, named Patricia. They called themselves homesteaders.

Being a homesteader was hard work. They had to clear huge stumps out of the way to make gardens.

They hauled endless buckets of water from the river, and spent hours chopping wood to keep their cabin warm.

It rained more in Quatsino Sound than Lilian thought possible. Every night, as she lay in bed, wolves howled outside the cabin.

When she wasn't working, Lilian found
time to take photographs of her life as a
homesteader.

She photographed cows and goats in
the fields, zucchini and tomatoes in their
gardens, and the boats they used to catch
fish and to get around.

Lilian loved being far away from cities and crowds. But, living in a forest with no roads, there was one thing she missed. She still loved cars and driving!

So one summer, Lilian, Charles, Patricia, and their pet blue jay took a road trip to California. Lilian drove their Ford Model T. To Lilian, the open road was freedom.

Years later, Patricia died from a disease called tetanus. Lilian was so heartbroken that she decided to move back to England by herself. She lived in a big house on a cliff where she watched the waves and the beaches below. She gardened, painted, and played the stock market.

As the years went by, most people forgot about Lilian's early adventures: her journalism career, her daring horseback riding, and her amazing flight in *Mayfly*. But nearly 100 years after that first flight, a few people began to celebrate Lilian's memory.

Today, Lilian is remembered as the first woman to design, build, and fly a plane. She is featured in museums in Ireland and Canada. A park in Northern Ireland is named after her. It has a big metal model of *Mayfly* to celebrate her bravery and freedom.

Lilian lived during a time when women didn't have as much freedom or as many opportunities as men. But Lilian didn't let this, or anything, hold her back from living life her own way. She never stopped trying to find her freedom.

HISTORICAL TIMELINE

1878
SEPTEMBER 28: Lilian is born in Maidstone, Kent, England.

1903
DECEMBER 17: Orville and Wilbur Wright become the first people in the world to build and fly an airplane. Their plane is called *Wright Flyer*.

1909
JULY 25: Louis Blériot, a French aviator, inventor, and engineer, becomes the first person to fly across the English Channel. His flight may have inspired Lilian to build her own plane.

OCTOBER 22: Raymonde de Laroche is thought to be the first woman to fly an airplane, built by French aviator Charles Voisin.

1910
Lilian designs and builds *Mayfly*.

AUGUST 31: *Mayfly* makes its first successful flight (about 400 metres) in County Antrim, Northern Ireland. Lilian becomes the first woman in the world to design, build, and fly an airplane.

1911
OCTOBER 3: Lilian marries Charles Loftus Bland.

1912
Lilian and Charles immigrate to Canada. They settle in Quatsino Sound on northern Vancouver Island and become homesteaders.

1913
APRIL 13: Lilian and Charles's only daughter, Patricia, is born.

1929
SEPTEMBER: Patricia dies of tetanus.

1932
MAY 20–21: Amelia Earhart becomes the first woman to complete a solo flight across the Atlantic. (She had completed an earlier transatlantic flight as part of a three-person crew, in 1928.)

1935
Lilian leaves Canada and returns to the United Kingdom, settling in Kent.

1971
MAY 11: Lilian dies in Sennen, Cornwall, England.

HALEY HEALEY is a high school counsellor, registered clinical counsellor, and the bestselling author of *On Their Own Terms: True Stories of Trailblazing Women of Vancouver Island, Flourishing and Free: More Stories of Trailblazing Women of Vancouver Island,* and *Her Courage Rises: 50 Trailblazing Women of British Columbia and the Yukon.* A self-proclaimed trailblazing woman herself, she has taught in isolated fly-in communities, guided whitewater canoe expeditions, and is happiest outdoors. She has an avid interest in wild places and unconventional people.

KIMIKO FRASER is an illustrator and historian-in-training. She grew up constantly making—drawing, painting, knitting, sculpting, book-binding, etc.—and has never learned how to stop. She is the illustrator of *Her Courage Rises: 50 Trailblazing Women of British Columbia and the Yukon.* She holds a bachelor of arts (honours History, major Visual Arts) from the University of Victoria. She works with many mediums to create her illustrations, including watercolour, digital, ink, and tea. Most of her work is inspired by her interest in plants, history, and folktales.